RINGS OF GREEN

Rings of Green

ANNE PETERS

COLIN SMYTHE
Gerrards Cross 1982

Copyright © 1982 by Anne Peters
First published in 1982 by Colin Smythe Limited
Gerrards Cross, Buckinghamshire

ISBN 0-86140-124-7
0-86140-129-8 Pbk

*British Library Cataloguing
in Publication Data*

Peters, Anne
Rings of green.
I. Title
821¹.914   PR6066.E73/

*Printed in Great Britain by
Skelton's Press Ltd., Wellingborough, Northamptonshire*

Contents

Acknowledgement is made to the Editors of the following anthologies and magazines in which some of these poems first appeared. *Poets of Today, The Gardener's Book of Verse, Poetry Ireland Review, Irish Press, Reality, Planet, Manifold, Spirit, America.*

The Haunted Dream

After the dream, after the plan
and sober calculation
came the execution of it all.
'What stalked through the Post Office?'

Yeats would have Pearse summon
'Cuchulain to his side.'
Myth and reality like harpstring and stone,
are part of each man's song and home.

But must reality be ruthless killing,
red blood splashed on stone and leaf,
blackening now our hapless 'rose'?
Must consequence disfigure dream?

Christ carried neither spear nor sword.
He begged forgiveness for his foes.
God, bestow the herb 'self-heal'
and help bind up our bleeding history.

Antiphon I

The Lord is my strength.

Who works in the wind
and diminishes dark
and swims with the trout upstream
works in me.
I call welcome to Cuan the hound
loping by wild flags
flowering yellow.
I am one with the young wind
coming by,
making willow strands tumble.
Light dancing
on the Lusk's ruckled waters
dances in me.

The Lord is my strength
and with my song I give Him thanks.

Antiphon II

Let all the earth sing.

Yes, even in the nature of dumb things
song is. You've heard
rain strumming on backs of rivers.
Listen to a locomotive speeding, wheels
stroking carols over metal of tracks.
And on this warm afternoon
waves whisper along sands
where winter brings the water cry of loon.

Let all the earth sing;
sing praise to Your Name.

Kevin O'Culihain Zorro Tio of the Andes

Ah, well! In the great Empire of all
I shall know the why
that fixed for me to be out away,
a shaun putting up poles
over the spines of the Andes
to carry the wires
to put lights in towns and huts
and power the mines.

And now
with the frost come over my fox-red hair –
I am known
across the Bolivian plateaus,
height upon height, by mule drivers,
ancianos and workers
as Zorro Tio – Fox Uncle –
worker of big magic,
an engineer.

But I was reared back there
where Great-Grandad's thatched house
is founded on the down-sloped hills
tucked between hedges, face to the sea,
weathering the noon sun
and the mist-laden winds.
O, I long to leave these snows,
for Ardaghloe,
for our green island.

Yes! 'Tis the beat of your seas
emerald and endless and full of whip
and the weep of your rains
that sing, ring and live in me always,
in spite of this dry-grit-in-teeth
snow height brood of abyss-built towers,
and the sight of your hills

with the lambs nuzzling cosy in the heather
and the red, red deer –
offspring of the wild red deer
that King Malachy hunted for food –
the same walking safe, without fear
like children playing ball
in your green, green greens
and the parks in the spitting breeze
and the sheen of the sun
and the peace, even in the dark
and porter-smelling pubs,
and the old, quiet or complaining,
and the rest, groaning or dreaming,
and the sea bordering you all
that keeps the love inside me.
And, if in the end I fail to get back,
when lifted and healed in the clean clear
won't all my wants
be the more perfectly fulfilled
for the forces tearing at me now? . . .

After Spring Rains

I breathe green rumours
in the air.
Grassblades bud with drops of rain.
The pear tree leans
rinsed against the blue.

The sun of spring rides higher.
Yellow clothes the naked willow.
Ruffles of scillas
and fiddlehead ferns
billow over my wild east corner.

Now after the startle of water-light,
the foxglove looks like the lily
and lilies light up like stars.
The pigeon struts like the peacock
and peacocks flirt like larks.

Looking toward the River

On All Soul's night you went.
Now long days begin, rosemary,
tanzy and camomile open playgrounds
for bees, a wind moves
among the new leaves, and I lean
on the summerhouse sill,
remembering the frost of that evening
in the herb garden's diamond dimness.

But I felt warm because I walked beside you,
as you told story on story
of your journey with fellow workers,
in heat and freezing rains,
up over Gilboa passes to the Moab plateau,
seeing cheetahs, vipers, wild boar,
jackals, and turpentine trees
strong as the oak that caught Absalom.

I look toward the river,
but the water is absent at sea,
leaving pools in the mud flats
where sandpipers flit
like tea-coloured butterflies.
Again in memory your voice speaks.
Were not the brackish waters of Mara
made wholesome by the touch of the Tree?

In the distance where my eyes
go searching for you
two swans float jubilantly white.
Kindly the incoming tide covers
the mud of the river. The garden
is alive with birdsong and the ripple
of water flowing into reeds.
Surely you can hear the expectant music?

Evening

Everything outside the house seems
just as it used to be before that storm;
only the wren's nest
is empty of bustle, robbed
by the Roche boy from over the way.
Now with evening, the walls,
the dead-light closes in;
unalterable hours dragging
the last times of your love out of focus,
and your burial ground
some spot on the cold seabed
beyond reach, beyond clocks, beyong dreams.
And the thud of the rains forever falling
and cars rolling up and down
the road – world without end.

A Wife's Lament

As snow dropped down last night
it covered the parched site
of our half-built house.
It put its unrelenting wrap
around shrunken holly roots,
and packed its frosted folds
along the sodded green, where only yesterday
they laid you.
Dear God, I'm hammered, broken, crushed.
How can I struggle with winds,
find shifts by which to choose
what way to turn or what to do,
with nothing in this world to wish for?

My beloved, my other half,
in death did the window open?
Open wide to solitude, fires unknowable?
Are there any fuchsia hedgerows
winding red about the city?
Do the bluebird pair bring their weightless shapes
to splash in Blessed Mary's spring?
And do the sky's mists hold brown throstles singing
for Mary's ear.

Yes, my sorrow, I remember
there is neither midday nor midnight,
there's no hour whatever
in that stretching of marvels
away on the rock mountain of heaven.
And I hear you say – as if you were here –
open the beehive door, my girl,
go into the fresh and plentiful air,
for honey-eyed days are coming
when you'll hear deep songs
drawn from the rushing sounds

of valleys flooding
and the pale buds venturing out
as spring laps over the land
in soft green waves.

But now, the hulk of night moves off
through snow clinging to blade and branch,
clean as the priest's white funeral bands.
Still the flakes fall, so quiet
their unruffled calm increases the tumult
of a mind
anguished by loneliness.

Snowlight

Hush, snow is falling, gentle, quiet,
garden, trees, church and spire
are veiled from view by fine spun skeins
tossed like spray off sky lagoons,
nothing so white as chill-born snow.

In the shivering silence of early morning,
the snow stops falling, garden,
trees, the wide expanse to distant hills,
present a world embalmed in white.
The silvered light is new, is new.

Progressions

Many now
are heedless mercenaries
who make the green belts in our cities
false lanes, hideouts for castaways,
lonely tunnels for lovers.
Their machines burn the air we breathe,
and pour deadly wastes into rivers and oceans
until there is no seaweed
left in the surrounding surf.
No spirit there.
People are tricked, they say,
by fast computer feed-ins.
And our language is going bankrupt
with words wrung thin
as the clicking of clocks.

Many more
are alert to the earth's great balances,
to the groans vibrating like buried cellos
from the rasps of our ignorances and progressions.
And surely there is purpose in change,
as creative force
shakes out powers, passions, and unfamilar music?
Would not the human spirit languish
were men to stop welding symbols,
signaling beyond the edges of truth
for further truths,
working down in the cold water-world's pressure
toward the unknown,
climbing beyond the fields of midsummer heat
that folds into the creamy calyx of the tuberose?

The Call

After my life's apprenticeship,
death circles about me, circling
slow as a rook coming home.
Fragrant as hyssop,
spikenard or myrrh, the sacramental oils,
moist, cool on my skin
trace a miraculous pattern
to restore first innocence.
Filled with vibrations of everything
once lived, loved, endured,
I turn to face the dark unknown.

Death but marks our mortal stretch.
Soul's thirst, mind's fear struggle
as the invitation to a journey unfolds,
the words flickering like flames
suspended on the wind's gentleness.
Soon, as though beckoned by a finger
my being, leaving its consort shape
to time, travels on.
I follow a path like a lighthouse beam
and come to a cave in a mountain top,
a place where the identity
I dread to lose can stay forever.

Looking out, I see wisdom on heights
of darkness, clothed in radiance of sapphire,
subdued as pearl
born of ocean, moon, and light.
She is the queen with ring and sceptre
walking on winds of wild white thyme.
She is the compassionate-eyed girl
searching neglected commons
for the ascension of trees.
She is the child

kneeling by the fountain of waters,
serious with green listening.

The sight dissolves in a scald of tears,
and torn with longing for the wholly other,
I loose from my back
the sacks of particular memories,
powers, failures, passions, dreams,
and discarding all but the satchel of self,
start down a trail
hemmed by hills of burning gorse.

Past the burning,
down the gorge, darkness grows.
I must race beyond fear, beyond death.
Sound swells resonant as ocean tides,
and off in the gloom a rift opens, white,
a shaft of milk-light.
Can it be the gate to an unimaginable city,
the needle's eye,
or a gap through which flood waters fall,
clean as tumbling snows?

Down at the end of that black descent,
a cataract looms,
swirling shawls of silken foam
into a fathomless pit. On the domes
no sentinel beacon flares,
no trumpet summons
vies with the boisterous roar,
but in the turbulence of water tones,
a call, gentle, clear,
spoken by an inimitable voice.
'Come! Love is my name,' it says.

Shedding the satchel,
the cherished last of self,
I will climb the rungs of the rapids.
Into the churning waves I plunge
and the mad waters wrap my slightness around.
Drowning in silvered wet,
as in a crystal glass
I see my soul, the spark of its inmost core
shining through the web-like layers
my life had spun. Aching, passionate
to reach the one who called,
I grasp an outcrop rock. In that instant,
loosed from the flood,
borne through boundless emptiness,
I am set, bankrupt, naked,
on the cobbled gap of knowledge.

In the given silence there is justice
and I find mercy.
Light flowers out of a brilliance of cloud
and in the white serenity
mind fired, and heart on fire,
I await the breaking moment
overleaping death
to the unending beginning in you,
O God!

Back there the Hills

Here am I, boss of Don Rudolph's Mines
and only two close kin are left at home,
my widowed sister Ellie and Uncle Taigh.
She writes that her five children
need five hundred things
and the land is let out for grazing,
being without a man.

Working under the Sierra of the Crowns,
I swear mildly, ears tightening against
din of crashing ore and shovel, alert
to the moods stirring among my Indian costaleros,
aware that age-old taboos need but the snap
of a spark to flare to disaster.

The long shift ended, the men
come out of the torn mouth of Towanaku,
breathing hard; but as fish gasping death-in-air
revive if thrown back into water,
so out in the frigid hyalite they quicken
down the steep to the company huts, muttering,
begging pardon of Patcha-Mama
for robbing her bone and womb.

Well, it's the truth
that these Andes are the greater size
where the winds whirl gales of ice,
and their summits stab the clouds like outsized spears.
It is from some spot in the towers below
Hanz and Rodrico's bodies
will get up when time ends
and the last dawn's golden cockcrow rings.

Back there the hills face up like toys
the Mighty One scattered down

to mould the various provinces
and zone the winding roads and waterways
that are the landscapes where my island's swans
fly high, close wings, and trumpet loud
before they conceal themselves and die.

But it isn't time
for me to turn about and go there yet
and it would seem
maybe that time won't come soon.

Double Storm

Night and a storm wind blows
over my island house as the waves
roll over the undertow, skirling froth.
The driftwood fire burns fitfully.
Where shall I go to escape
the blue sea-serpents that lurk
in the caves of the cliffs and glide
through the crannies of my mind?

Like a tinkling bell
my ease loving self produces
distractions: a man on a dragon horse
with a pearl in its mouth,
turkeys gobbling cryptic noises
by the well at Cormac's chapel,
a red plumed bird tied to a vine
hung with clusters of tinsel grapes.

The forms subside as words rise
from the unfathomable centre of life.
Let go the playful baubles,
such things are props less real
than fog wreaths on Ben Bulben,
reckon with the myths of horsemen,
draw wisdom from the chapel's well.
Love locked up dies like a caged linnet.

Morning. The baleful wind becomes demure
lazily drawing begonia light
over the dark. The sea gives up its wrath.
The storms could well have been
but wraiths in the crotchets of my skull.
I wade to the mainland on a ridge
of seawrack, rock and mussel shells
made by God's grace into a crossing.

Presentiment in Beauty

There is a look on the face of the country,
the look that comes on a gleamy morning.
There is a gloss on the fields
like the sheen of silk.
Smooth as glass the river flows
to break in liquid white on stones.

A kingfisher sits on a willow bough
motionless above a pool.
Flash of sapphire-green as it drops
to the water and minnow in beak
streaks down stream.

Leisurely as a toy ship in a lazy wind,
a butterfly with peacock wings
alights on a thistlehead,
blind to the swallows that wheel and swoop
coalbright in the sun.

High in the blue transparency of sky
glint of steel as a jet-plane glides
swifter than eagle, sleek as a fish,
triumph of man's technology,
dependent on him for energy and aim.
Can it presage a land where no bird flies?

The Rains

The day's last rays loiter
over Black Mountain,
as the lake's lavender creases
drop into shade. And I, hearing the wind
among the orchard's green cradles
like the sobbing of babies,
remember hugging my own baby, dead,
as if love could give her life.

With the taste of salt on my lips
I cried to God for help,
and heard but the mourning tones of a dove,
and a shiver of leaves
behind the flight of a startled bird.

I knelt by her cot, frozen
of feeling as the moon's pale sickle
mirrored in the lake, and dressed
my small stranger in muslin and lace,
a white shroud like our alyssum.

Now, having drawn these memories
out of hiding at last,
I know that called or not called
God is there.
The sound of the wind has stopped grieving.
Clouds melt to rain, showering
dry roots and valleys.
There is a cure in many waters.

At Daybreak

All about our home, the chestnut trees,
rocks, saxifrage and gypsywort
wait, hooded in night,
ready to disclose their faces
as the gannet-feathered shadows swerve.
A rose-fired spot unfurls
sifting lilac on white,
and dour yet the stone knolls
like knuckled fists butt over the slope
where tall cedars thrive,
less than Lebanon's but our own.

Dawn widens its long cornice
and soon, behind the trees
Foley's men will start again
blasting the far side of Stranlough Ridge.
Odd how quick its granite hump shrinks,
and I remember Molly wrote
her uncle's farm was brindled
with roadside rubble,
and Bill Whelan, fishing
up near Castle Dalton, found axe blades
like sharks biting among the beeches.

Bruised, cold in heart and bone
I'd sealed me down. Yet even now
I notice colour flashes
breaking into sound, the redbreast
pitching his homestead challenge
from the crabapple top,
the pheasant's blare
a gimlet curling up the elm,
a flock of yellow wagtails flickering
gold as dandelions
in the glaze of our patch-pocket pond.

And as I watch, the lilac gloom
turns topaz; the cedars,
and the hill-backed fields
all catch the awakening fire,
intensifying amber, rose, and white,
burning the chill out of my wounded mind.

Legacies of Light

I am a structure of mended bones,
a damaged man
wrapped in grafted skin,
with eyes that see no more
but the fires that live in the dark,
remembrances that are part
of the time before the sun died.
The indestructible things,
the legacies of light
shine sharp-cut among the minor prisms
and prosaic flotsam in my store.
Then there are fears, inexplicable,
haphazard bits, as in sleep
where night spirits hover
like bat-wings in a narrow cave.
Yet there is mercy in survival,
and on days like this
as the first thunder of the year
stops rumbling, fancy is fired
to watch divided April
streaking north, north-east
on sun brushed paths to where clouds
start raining, furlongs of liquid
to coax blue irises awake
before summer raises
gold-leaf days to bleach hay,
to scent carnations, and shape
new praises within my shuttered dark.

As Bombs Devour now One and now Another

In Lebanon by a dry stream bed
on Zghorta hill
the mother of Ephraim sat,
five smooth pebbles clenched in her fist.
Across the mulberry and olive groves
came the tolling of church bells –
the alarm – slow as the rolling of boulders
over an iron hard slope.

But the woman sat rigid
as the withered stump she leaned against.
Wind bitter in the slender olive leaves,
air tainted by the reek of terror's aftermath,
a flock of crows like a dusky cloud
moving unhurried on its accustomed way.
Ephraim, my son,
never again will my ears tingle
to your voice,
my feet quicken to your footsteps.

A bomb, they had said,
and not even a jacket button left.
Ephraim, my son, my son,
why did you have to go?
Lifting her fist she hurls the pebbles
at the dried up water course.
Five puffs spurt from the earth,
fleeting feathers of dust.

Light in Darkness

At Peking's triple-domed Temple of Heaven
Fu-jen clutches her fingers –
when a spirit parts from its body
a light is seen travelling, swift;
high as a crane flies,
it goes,
leaving the sky empty.
What happens, Lord Buddha,
when the man is killed by hand of man?
In the night,
moonshine on the shadow-bamboo shoots
glitters black.

On the Third Day

Toward morning after the Sabbath,
the wind turned violent, uprooting
mustard, bitter herbs, and desert broom.
Lightning ripped the dark,
glinted on the spears of soldiers
guarding the tomb. The earth trembled
and the great stone door rolled back.

Then lapped by sunrise flame
slowly the torn, grey landscape
floated out of the dark. In that instant,
as though touched by an angel,
springs welled on barren heights,
rose-shaped flowers of myrrh
glowed pink on rock and sand,
wild iris luminous lemon and orchid-blue
unfurled by the waterbrooks.

A man walked in a garden.
Washed by light the long grey leaves
of the olive trees shimmered.
Birds sang glad praises to the sun.
Bees flew toward the flowering of their desire.
And Magdalene ran, radiant with the news
of the Crucified One. His return.

The Daughter of Lir
for Joseph O'Higgins

In the studio of his barrack-like house
by the sea front, he worked, absorbed,
as under the influence of his hands
shaping the clay,
the blocked-out head, sweep of neck,
and shoulders of a young girl grew.

I, his student model, sat motionless,
my thick tweed coat small armour
against the chill of a fireless room,
damp as the sea-sprayed quays outside.
Professor O'Higgins they all called him
in Youghal. A tall man
in loosely fitting clothes,
black hair bristling around his head.
During rest periods he taught me to roll
the slippery clay into pellets
and apply them to my skeleton study of a foot.

More often there would be quiet,
punctuated only by his fits of coughing.
But sometimes he stopped work
to stroll about, lift the wet cloth
off his rough of a sleeping child,
or halt by his bust of a fisherman,
point out how to catch
the marks of age in the bend of a head,
line of skull, or he would begin to talk
of bygone worlds of Ireland.

His voice would start soft,
tracing back myths, folklore,
and supersititions, and take on a glow –

the poetry of the people, their solace
around the peat fire of an evening.
He told of Ogham, the God of Eloquence,
and Brigit, the three-fold Muse.
But best I loved to hear about the Old Tribes
strong in knowledge of tree magic.
The Rowan, 'Delight of the Eye,'
its flame-coloured berries holding power
to heal wounded warriors.
And the secret of the Fern
with well-hidden seed growing in shade,
the magic of which made a borrower invisible.

II

Today after Mrs. O'Higgins brought the tray,
as I sipped the hot tea,
he went to the window
watchful as a sailor reading the signs
of ocean and cloud,
'Listen to the wind
rising with the incoming tide,' he said.

Indeed wind and wave were in flight together,
like warning voices,
the dark tumult of the waves
pounding the sea wall,
and the wind crying in the black-armed yew trees.
Across the bay a line of swans,
stretched lean as a skein of silk,
china white against the green,
flew in toward the reed flats.
'Lir's children.
Nine hundred years was the term of their exile.'

Once started, he told of the crime
when jealousy of her step-daughter, Finola,

and step-sons, Aed, Fiacre, and Conn,
took root in the heart of Eva.
From the Palace under the hill
she drove them to a desolate lake
and made them bathe.
As each child entered the water
she struck with her magical wand
transmuting their shapes to swans.
'No power of Lir or Druid can now save ye
from endless wandering the Seas of Erin
with shrieking gulls and fishy seals.'

With that, he turned
and snatching up a lump of clay,
thrust bits onto the shoulder curves,
like a man seized by an outside power.

I pose again, chin slightly tilted,
with a confusion of thoughts going in
and out, half glimpsed reflections
of steam ships, swans, and strange horizons.
Here is home, the old town, its streets
straggling up and down the hill,
the fishermen mending their nets by the quays,
where one knows, or partly knows
the people, and is partly known.
Only days before I go away.
If only it were a dream. Step-children.
Bird-shaped but with their own natures,
banished to the Seas of Moyle and Inis Glora.
Nine hundred years.
How many years before I can get home?
How can I tell him?

When the sitting ended, after I'd pulled
on my woollen cap and scarf, I waited,
eyes on the floor, loath to speak.

'What's troubling you, child?' he asked.

'Can you finish your portrait without me?'
I blurted, 'for soon I must be gone away.'

'Where are you going?'

'To Boston. To work in an aunt's hat shop.
She's paid the steamship ticket.'
A spasm of coughing shook the length
of his bony thinness. A handkerchief
pressed to his mouth; red on the linen
showed bright as the blood
of a wounded bird fallen on snow.

'For too long the country has been deprived,'
he frowned, 'with the young going,
emptying the land of her children's breath,
leaving her without poets, teachers,
without strong workers, lovers.
God knows, once they had small choice,
but nowadays . . .' his voice trailed off,
a hand lifting as if to question.

'I-I have to go. It's all fixed.'

Covering his sculpture, carefully he tucked
the damp sheet about it and smiled at me.

'It's coming, alannah, it's well on the way.'

III

After the crisis leaving Ireland,
the 'leap in the dark' across the Atlantic,
dying a little daily of loneliness,
daily too – a greenhorn – I discover

new words, new ways, new delights,
the greater shine and heat of summer,
the weeping in the music of the black people.

Now it is the fall of the year.

Not paved with gold, these streets,
but carpeted with leaves,
and on stands in Harvard Square, the peaches,
pumpkins, pears, and green-sheathed corn,
such fruits of perfect shape
and hue I had never seen.
After work I drift along
air warm with the scent of apples.
Neither hedge nor wall lend privacy
to the homes of wood, not stone,
unforeseen and attractive.

In my lodgings, a black edged envelope,
addressed to me, strange handwriting.
Who could have died? I stand awhile.
Recent letters from the family said
they were all well,
except for Uncle Edward's heart.
Finally I took it out to the back veranda,
sat on the steps and tore it open.

Ah, it is from Joseph O'Higgins.
'A Chara,
            There is pleasant news,' he wrote.
'My bust of a Youghal Fisherman
won a gold medal at the Paris Exposition.
My other entry, the portrait for which you sat,
got an honourable mention,
not as a girl of the present day
but as The Daughter of Lir.
On firing, the clay turned a good brown

and is hard as stone.
But the Daughter of Lir should be of bronze.
If ever, no, when you do come back, alannah,
will you see to it?
I believe it worthy,
so leave it to you, who shared in the making.'

Huddled on the vine-shaded steps,
I read and reread
Mrs. O'Higgins's accompanying note.
Tuberculosis.
Forty, not so very old. Through pressure
of unshed tears I see as in a crystal sphere
the living O'Higgins, bent
intently working,
entangled with a backdrop of flying swans,
the flowing green
of Mull Head sinking into the water.

Thud of a fallen apple where the maples
drown the slender tree in shadows.
From the house comes faint music.
For no reason
it reminds me of an Aran prayer:
'The light of heaven to his soul.'

Protect her, Lord,
and tell him, please, I will get back.
I will see to the bronze.
                              I promise.

Flights

After a life of hours
sewing sleeves, sewing dresses
in the incessant bicker of needles,
I step into commuter throngs
surging between skyscapers
like pebbles in an ebb-tide.

Back in the kingdom of my room,
I glimpse a plane against the blue
where jets, racing sound,
streak the horizon's curve,
and I dream the old dream
to sail at ease upon the air –
go the way a herring gull
that coasting over surf
alights on moon-white sands.

No, I fly the tumbling ocean
strong-winged as a shearwater
fighting trade winds,
banking on wave troughs, springing
on air-flows to the rough slopes
of the irregular island,
fleece of pine trees compact as carpets,
golden stooks and tilting grasses
a furlong below.

Abruptly the dream-flight ends.
Sound explosive as thunder
drowns ears,
stuns consciousness.

In the lull a dog howls.
I reassure myself, only a sonic boom,
and mind outsoars all birds.

Green fire in my bones
unrestrained by manufactured time,
upon a single sigh
I jet the full three thousand miles –
home.

The Listening Heart

There is a voice that is hard to deny.
It may be only the breath of a whisper,
the sound of wind in piny heather.
The spirit speaks to the listening heart,
to the one who hearing of the treasure
hidden in the field and being resolute
goes simply as the child Fion,
who tiptoes past the cromlech stone
searching for the honeycomb
he believes the bees have stored
in the wild grape vine along the wall.

Out of the Night

The well is deep behind our eyes
where mysteries lodge by day
and rise into the twilit sphere
between sleeping and waking.
Through the first sliver of dawn
I see a heron standing motionless
among reeds by a mist covered lake.
A cloud of butterflies drifts
above a friar in a shabby brown habit
holding a wolf's paw in his hand.

Out of the dream I come
as if counselled by angels,
and find all things transformed,
greener trees, sweeter air,
and finding myself other than the one
who lay down to sleep, I'm off
to follow the way of the saint
who tamed his brother the wolf with love,
and blessed his little sister the lark
who listened as he prayed.

They can close the post offices,
I will confide my letters
to the rapid runnels of rivers.
They can close the banks,
I will pull silver dollars
out of the seas' counting houses.
I will disown clocks.
I will be as that motionless heron
watching for the signs and mysteries
beneath the shadowed surfaces of the world.

The Forest Door

As a wood-dove moves
through the orchard grasses,
the city boy sprawls
on a leaf-screened tilt of ground,
chewing a hazelnut twig.

Catching the snap of brittle stalks,
he rises on one cautious knee
and sights the smoke-mauve head.
He mistakes it,
shadowy as the ancient days,
with a story he'd read.
'It's the King's own hawk,'
he thinks, his lips near whistling.

The hawk firmly held on the Kingly wrist
is slipped from its hood,
soars till it is but a speck in the sky
and circles to 'wait on'
the game being flushed,
then arching in headlong dive
it strikes its prey
and a magpie falls in a fury of feathers.

The pictured story flips aside,
for suddenly the dove takes off,
its winnowing wings breaking the air
as if loud in fright, and the boy jumps up
to watch its flight.

But seeing a butterfly
perched on a weed,
he hesitates,
and when a piebald pony
stops to look over the fence

with friendly gaze and twitching ears,
the boy forgets
the allure of the hawk he thought he'd seen.

Ah! Loving, giving, seeing . . .
the orchard is for the boy the forest door
to sharing in the everlasting kingdom
of the fields,
where the land is overrun with green,
where strange things are real,
and the wind smells of cider
and apples are the gift of trees.

Moon Goddess

Is the Moon-goddess
Aine of Munster,
bartering silver for amber?

Is she hopefully fishing
for trout like the Princess Dechtire
who swallowed a may-fly
and brought forth Cuchulain?

Is the ray of love bruised in her
as in a peach
which the Sow-goddess tramples,
or is she held hostage
watched by the Black Cat of Clough?

Is she Brigit goddess of poets
singing airs
to the harps of Muirthemne,
or is she asleep in the tower
at Mac Coll's winter castle?

Perhaps we can find that goddess
as she moves
silver gowned through the night.

May Goddess

Is Olwen the Flower-goddess
daughter of Hawthorn,
formed from nine blossoms
from whose airy footprints
white trefoil springs up?

Is Olwen the Love-goddess
quince bough in hand,
enthroned on Caer Idris
confiding her secrets
to poets who love her?

Is Olwen Blodeuwen
bride promised to Llew
Lord over Gwynedd,
guarded by watch dogs
in the woods of Celyddon?

Is Olwen Queen Cardea
disguised as a bird,
circling the universe
sky, earth and water
with her twin brother Merdinn?

Is Olwen the white goddess
whom you might see in May,
casting spells with the hawthorn
as she follows the cuckoo
or chases the hare?

Glimmerings

On such a clear dark moonless night
from where I stand outside the house
the stars seem new
as they used to look when I was young.
Again I have the childish thought
that they are salamanders' eyes,
and knots of marcasite,
sprays of glassy flowers
with light locked in.
Up there beside the Milky Way
how bright Orion's Belt and Sword!

But who set suns and galaxies
to float on patterned courses?
What mind conceived their scale,
and for earth designed a 'sphere of breath'
for lack of which the moon is dead?
One, I would say,
who loving colour, light, and shade,
gave sky's blue to bluebells
growing under trees,
and to the glow-worm emerald sparks
to attract the flying male.

Rings of Green

About the contours of the mound
three ramparts wind,
giant steps toward the summit,
steep sided and high,
watered by our island's weather.
Here in this earthen stronghold,
dwelt people of the 'Middle Kingdom'.

Time has tailored these acres surely.
Gone are the woods that sheltered
the red deer of the mountain.
No more the Druids' hallowed groves.
Near a fern circled rock,
blue-green shadows stretch
from a whitethorn, ash, and oak,
trees sacred to the company of spirits.
A train whistles at a distant crossing,
machines carve up the land for roads.
Yet last November the boy Turlough saw
the mound ablaze with moving lights,
crystal white and fiery red,
like satellites of Moon and Mars.

Who is to call what Turlough saw
unreal? Who knows
what eternal currents flow
about the precincts of a place,
around three rings of green,
or what can open one man's eyes
to emanations of past acts
in war or peace, despair or joy?

Celebration

Walking from the candlelight,
beatitude within sanctuary walls,
out into the early cold,
companion-strangers
we share the seal of blessed ashes,
residue of palm and fire,
beautiful
in the brief passion of dissolution.

Away we hurry, hiding
human fears, doubt, desires,
like oysters sheltering parasites and pearls.
A robin's song assails the morning gloom.
The wind shifts,
a spring swirl of dust celebrates
what is done and to come
between bleak stone and some far leaf-green land.

The Voice of the Owl

In the woodland lane
the earth is cold,
hard as tortoise-shell.
Only the crunch of my footsteps
breaks the winter quiet.
Pain, remorseless
as the doctor's verdict,
robs me of breath.
What looms before me fills my mind.

Then a cry,
long and clear, a plaintive cry,
tremulous as a note
blown on an old hunting horn.
It is an owl,
gliding on its noiseless flight.
Like lens set for certain signs
its glaring eyes
probe dark verges and black dykes.

At the sound of its call,
the mouse by its hole,
the vole by the pool,
the sparrow in the ivy, freeze.
My thoughts ride ahead of my feet.
I remind myself
man is more than his body, with death
but the passover to becoming
totally other.

Again the owl, its beautiful, strange
long, quavering song
flowing back through icy branches.
Blessed be the perilous owl,
blessed be adder, goose, and badger,

blessed be every lurking,
hunting, flying creature.
Exalted be night for stars,
for danger, and varying light.

Hidden Fire

Dwelling
        in the hollow of time,
Measure
        of Now in the eye of God,
Each Life
        imbued with an inimitable force,
Contained
        as tranquil fire,
Glows
        in the wounds of the Word.

Spirit of Evil

It is night and the Night-Time Devil,
cold and faultlessly concealed,
goes about his unutterable job,
agitating the Back Bay waters in Boston,
busy in Peking,
sowing baneberry plants in Brazil.

Power of Darkness,
his face is nowhere to be seen
as he swirls about like a sable simoon,
buffets the brooding
blowing lotus pollen on our prides,
trying in the uproar to dim the light.

He creeps behind the lonely, whispering lies,
whistles his corruptive ditties
in the corridors of our desires,
roams streets, scouts taverns,
hating, but blandly solicitous,
trying to lower love.

Spirit of Evil,
he invades gardens, grafts seeds
of the mistletoe berry on the lime trees' bark,
pauses to cuff one sloe-eyed mouse
into the claws of the lynx
prowling under the backyard quince.

The Demon whose name is Legion
seeks to cut heart from mind,
nudges the grudges of nations, promoting
assassinations and night-flaring wars.
Yet tethered by the Lord
he fails to dim the Light.

Bones and Body

Last night my bones got up
and beckoned my body, but it remained
undone upon the bed.
The skeleton dancing by the door
might have been just white birch
embraced by twin winds.

It crept close and focused
its skull's empty gaze on me,
the sockets widening. In the depths
as if televised by the red-brown light
of an eclipsed moon, a shape loomed.
The vast clown form exuded power.

Dry trees crashed without sound,
on the heath figures irrupted,
thrust of pike met scythe, swords flashed.
Mute images of men dropped, beheaded.
Tall as gallowglasses
warriors got up, pulling helmets on.

Among the battling jousters
a gentle presence moves,
the hair molten as autumn evening,
catching the glint
of the warriors' helmets, bronze
in the red-brown blur of bodies.

Suffering the pantomine of unreason
I tried to think, were these
reflections of the primitive self,
of long forgotten combats,
embodiments of spirit powers,
love and hate jousting for room?

Drops of rain fell bitter as mourning.
I waited flesh-heavy upon the bed,
a tangle of plots flowing
over a face neither awake nor sleeping,
and the earth a copper acorn
slipping between sun and moon.

I waken in bright sunlight
to the sound of the alarm clock ringing.
My cheeks moist,
the tears my own. Casual
as breath and blood in life,
body, bones, self and soul are one.

Light Unfolds

At the beginning before he created man
God said, 'Let there be light,'
and light began.
Later man struck flint and made
his own, a fire destructive or benign.

And now the engineers confide
that they have found the laser,
a light like liquid glass tuned to flow
in jets straight as railroad tracks,
freighting in an instant flash
a thousand sounds and sights
through alpine airs and mackerel skies.
It also shoots a bullet of light, pin-pointed
as a hypodermic needle, so intensely hot
it punches holes in diamonds.

Holes – even Brother Jasper at Gethsemani
who prays to sleep and rise with Christ,
says he doesn't relish the idea
of being pierced by laser beams, ruby
or synthetic pink, whether in or out of tune.
But his spirits lift on being told
that research men predict
still thinner rays
'knives' able to treat a single cell
within the retina of an eye.

Beyond the laser's beam
there is the skitter of atoms,
invisible bees unifying matter.
Unknown forces wait to unfold
in a general drift toward a heightened end.

Nomad Day

Softly as an orange-tipped butterfly,
nomad day, bride to light, touches
the Irish hills and vanishes to the west.
Far out on the horizon, a rift of coral
lingers as dark drops over the ocean's pool.

Now, turning the key in dandelion gates,
light and day go hand in hand.
Cities' towers and thoroughfares
shed their neon diadems,
mountains and midsummer trees
spill dark like water from their shoulders.
The lovers' gaze goes gentle
about mighty pine and blue-starred grass.
Bird calls to bird, music running in
and out of shade, liquid as brooks lifting
and falling on harp-tones of pebbles.
Lychnis flames in crimson tides,
St. John's Wort offers
gold pomanders to grace the bride,
and costmary provides leaves
to sweeten the bridal washing waters.

Mad with day's splendours, light ties up
her hair with nets of trailing myrtle,
wraps her brightness in a violet cloud,
and sweeps her off to sleeping Asia.

A Chinese Painter

Turning from public death
and inward meditation, Pien Chou
transmits to changing silk
harmonies fragile as pollen,
trembling like a snow of dews,
whitening the blue
where immensity rests about a blackcap bird
ruffling its wings at dawn

Oriental Artistry

Sunset, the birches stand
against a glow of apricot light.
Nearby some chiff-chaffs flit about,
and the marmalade cat
with the cauliflower ear pauses,
body graceful in compression,
face flat with ambition
as becomes an expert at tight mischief.

I start, fists rap the window pane
as the cat springs and olive wings beat.
Prey twitching in his jaws,
the animal slinks off.
From a bush a tenant thrush whirrs up
into the last saffron crevice of day.

Lethal from jungle forests,
sagacious pets,
exponents of the double-life,
cats are born artists.
Two sleek models, a calm couple
sit on our chimney mantel.
They come from Canton
and are made of grey glazed china.

Eruption

Beyond the great plain,
in rocky woods where columbine nectar
nourishes long-tongued insects,
light quivers on crests of trees.
After the hush of night,
under the green-gold shade
sounds gentle as ripple of mountain streams.
Little birds wake,
warblers, vireos, purple finches.

Suddenly, as though hell erupted,
violence.

A bloated grey corolla coils skyward.
Fire leaps from tree to tree
while frenzy rages under burning spruce.
Screeching defiance a red-tailed hawk
flies from the blistering air.

Flames die on ember turf,
ash, fragments of misery float like feathers
torn from doves,
the wind sighs through blackened stumps,
wind over a lifeless land.

Absorbed in nuclear riddles
scientists brood.

Following snows and many rains
the streams are in their beds once more
burbling over stones.
Ghosts wailing in madness
go like thistledown in dreams.
Magenta fireweeds beautify the wounded earth

and cirrus clouds start the ceremony
of night to morning
over fresh young spires of spruce.

Avalanche

Stealthily the returning sun splits
the alpine dark, its flaming ball
and rose brushed rays
pouring light and heat on summits,
glaciers, chasms, frowning brows
and snow packed slopes
high above the valley of Chenaux.

Breakfast time in the ski lodge.
A great log fire burns on the hearth.
Multilingual voices mingle
lively as twelve-toned chords
debating depth and texture of the snow,
angles and hazards of diverse runs,
the cliffs, the woods of larch below.

Under the catalysis of the sun's glare
ice cracks, crevasses open.
Inch by inch dense masses of snow,
chunks of ice and stone
slide, exploding over the scarp.
The avalanche falls, a white cascade
gathering force as it rolls.

Its icicle tusks gouge boulders
and scree, the onrushing roar grows
as the great waves strike.
Down on the bottom the ground drum booms.
Slowly the brutal echoes quiet
leaving Chenaux, lodge and chalets
under a kill-weight of cold.

Ritual Costumes

Spring delights in masquerade,
fills the wind with yellow showers,
freshens rugs of shaggy moss
for childrens' feet on woodland trails.
In an hour conjures herbs,
fennel, vervain, trefoil leaves
to hinder witches of their will,
then colour-washing air with light,
trims the beech with quills of green
and hills with lenten-lily trumpets.

Summer comes with wild rose weather,
unfolds the kingdom's stores.
Textures fine as chinese silk
clothe fishspine stalks and crooked stems
with poppy, white, and turquoise hues.
Lengthening days join amber rains,
loop crimson fruits on bush and vine,
rouge the orchards' wan-cheeked peaches,
mix bryony and bittersweet,
candlegleams in hedgerow shrines.

Troubled Heritage

As she walked up the path from town
among the yellow gorse and bees,
counting, 'he loves me, loves me not,'
on a wild grain stalk, the sound of gunfire
shattered the quiet.
Swerving like a wounded creature
she stopped, breath held,
thin back pressed against a pillar stone.

Not so long ago waking to the curt rat-tat
of hunters' guns, her mind of fifteen
refusing the falling snipe,
or rabbit lying bloodied in the fern,
would shy away to gentler scenes.

Today burdened with a bitter heritage,
the hollows of her ears hold
noises tearing metal to pieces,
the flaming gasp of a Belfast building,
clatter of bullets on street walls.

Behind clenched lids
her eyes see wetness dark as bog pools
stain the pavement beside a man fallen,
and a woman stumbling toward him
amid a scatter of people.

Words welled, unbidden
as the heart throbs drumming in her blood.
God, O God pity, have pity,
them and us black with the hate festering deep and deeper
like an old sore . . . .
Beyond the cliffs the evening sun
a great yellow globe on a scarlet tide,
its fire eating into the sea.

Alternate Rhythms

Love and fury like the Great Clock pendulum
oscillate in our foetus' memory.
Under surface of events,
revolutions, fear, war,
an alternate rhythm beats.
Nurtured in cruel silence
love, faith, paradox
fuse the spendthrift energy of souls. Upward,
irrestible as gleam of swans in gloom,
some men and women,
rising on ghost-winged feet
conspire with the Spirit's grace
to open clouds,
to bless new paths with light.

Symbols of Harmony

At the felicitous moment
when beliefs were shared,
bowing with the breeze
blowing from the unknown fountainhead,
mason, carpenter, sculptor,
glassmaker, architect, painter
laboured together
grouping play of numbers
in soaring of pillars,
in Christs of painted wood,
irregularities of granite scrolls and gargoyles,
constructing marvels for their children
and for children yet unborn,
till the earth was garlanded
with diadems of churches.

To a Poet

Who is it
finds and ignites
the deeper hidden music
and fires flights
for the child-in-me
and for all other
St. John Wort lovers
who hear and, hearing
glimpse the violent unities?

Who is it
recalls the falcon's flights
and penetrates the frontiers
of my cart-tracked ears
to mount and journey into distance
over hills of cinnabar reds,
discovering lands with grottos
where the evening primrose grows
and late each May to find
ten thousand peonies,
spread beneath the core
of the furrowed sunset,
lifting up deep-coloured heads?

The Poet
walking in our rural woodland
when the brook was almost dry,
flung just one word to the stream.
And in the afterlull,
leaves dropped, each alone,
and under the Indian summer's heat
caught fire.

The Green Martyrdom

Brendan the Voyager, Bishop of Erin,
braving the angry currents
that hissed and coiled like snowy serpents
about rock-skirted Inishmore,
Inishturk, and Inishglora,
brought knowledge of Christ to pagan islanders.
After months of prayer in his homeland
he pushed his coracle ever further
battling the roar-rush of tides
to the rude lands of Alba, Britain and Gaul.
Great hardships of rowing, foundations
of monasteries and schools of learning.

Weary years later, after landing at Fenit,
he retired to his wind-swept hut
atop the cliff-sided peak of Mt. Brenainn.
Many signs, many omens opened visions
as he fasted on berries and water.
One evening, peace overflowing
from the solitude of stars untarnished
up in the sky heights,
he let thoughts follow each other like feet
striding through his mind, and imbued
by a spirit of penitence, he resolved to break
from all he loved and toil anew among strangers.

And it was morning. He pondered.
Barinthus had told of a vast land
of fruitful trees, herbs, and blossoms,
a paradise hidden behind the ice-mists,
lurking seabeasts, and water-spouting monsters
of the inhospitable Atlantic.
And did not the colonies of terns
that summered around the seaborders
fly away into the sunset each autumn?

Did not the brent-geese that wintered
in the flats and reed-beds of rivers,
fly off into the western horizon each spring?

As a white gull opens its wings
with a long cry before flight,
Brendan cried aloud:
'God of my brothers, strengthen me!'
Thus, in repentance, and for the sake of others,
he chose the green martyrdom of exile,
to seek the Land of Many Hues.
In a boat of oxhide, bitumen, and rosin,
back turned to Erin,
he started out across the unknown seas,
aiming toward the bright bed of the sun.

At the Clearing

Having travelled back to the country
of my beginnings, I climb the track
by the stream. The shrill zit-zit
of a dipper mingles with splash of water.
I look for worlds my child heart knew.
In woods the ruined tower has crumpled
and trees are sparse where whisper
and hue of fables flowed on wands
of rowan and pine. I saunter to a clearing
and sit against a grassy bank.
Now stone-still, as a spirit creature
drawn by witchcraft out of air, a hare
confronts me, brown-blue eyes on mine,
signature of earth and sky.
Long before cities, cars, and jet planes
our fathers ploughed these once wild lands
and hunted these fern-watered hills.
I sense the continuous patterns
that myth, history, and individuals weave,
as clouds exchange their shades
for thunder, rain or shining day.
A stir. The shy hare goes,
wingfooted across the changes.

The Long Agony

Blue as bellflowers,
the sky caps land and sea,
marred by dumpling clouds,
dark as turf stacks.

Her bicycle left
under the hawthorn hedge,
Breeda climbs Columba's Hill.
Having reached the top, she leans
against the wind-worn shrine.

'Power of the saints be with me now.
There's father killed,
Terence in prison. Liam missing.
Death is not nervous
met full tilt in the bullets' thin stream,
death is not the sorrow,
isn't it in the heartbreak of others,
scores of others,
isn't it in the waste?
Joan Mitchell legless.
The men bitter, stiffened in anger,
the ebbing of friendships.
Oh! Don't forsake us, Christ.
Christ, wash our hates away . . . .
terrible as we are.'

Eased, she watches the gulls' long swings
light and strong on the buffeting seawind,
breadth of endless ocean,
the horizon lifting in balconies of opal,
signs of the Mighty invisible.

A blast-burst in the air.
On the road below
black fumes of confusion spread
polluting the unploughed green.

Envoi

On the mind-day of one forever gone
I ask
for the sake of fathering rivers,
mothering earth,
pine trees, bog oaks, green revelations of seawaters,
fires of ruby,
symbols,
lavenders, snowdrops, asphodels,
for memory and forgetting,
for fulfilment of the learned and the simple,
for all things numbered and unnumbered,
for new sons,
come,
move us to expel our demons,
    end hatred   and
        come love
fire this waste of cinders
           come kingdom come.